easy origami ANiMALS

RUTH UNGERT

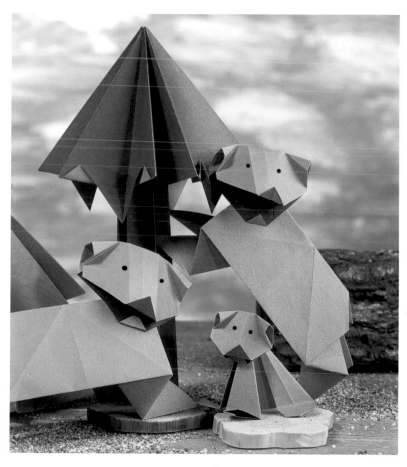

Sterling Publishing Co., Inc.   New York

Edited by Claire Bazinet
Photos by Frank Schuppelius

Library of Congress Cataloging-in-Publication Data Available

10 9 8 7 6 5 4 3 2 1

Published by Sterling Publishing Co., Inc.
387 Park Avenue South, New York, NY 10016
English translation © 2003 by Sterling Publishing Co., Inc.
Originally published under the title *Origami-Tiere für Kinder*
© English Publication GmbH, Wiesbaden 2001
Distributed in Canada by Sterling Publishing
C/o Canadian Manda Group, One Atlantic Avenue, Suite 105
Toronto, Ontario, Canada M6K 3E7
Distributed in Great Britain and Europe by Chris Lloyd at Orca Book
Services, Stanley House, Fleets Lane, Poole BH15 3AJ, England
Distributed in Australia by Capricorn Link (Australia) Pty. Ltd.
P.O. Box 704, Windsor, NSW 2756, Australia

Sterling ISBN 1-4027-0189-6

Contents
(Index of Zoo Denizens with Skill Ratings)

Skill Levels:
* = Beginner
** = Intermediate
*** = Advanced
**** = Expert

Preface

Origami, a Japanese term for the art of paper folding, is at least several hundred years old in Japan. It is believed, however, that paper folding actually began in China, which could mean that this art form has existed for more than a thousand years!

Besides the play and educational value of origami, and the restful enjoyment of simply crafting figures out of paper, origami is an important part of life in Japan. There, origami of all shapes and sizes are used in special ceremonies, as festive decorations, and displayed year-round in homes. With their deceptively simple and clean lines, traditional origami figures are both beautiful and inspiring.

Strictly speaking, traditional origami involves taking just a single square sheet of paper and—just by folding it—creating a complex, perhaps even three-dimensional, paper figure. This is a real challenge to one's imagination and geometrical ability, but it can produce real pieces of art. The use of only a single sheet, in fact, often results in not only a beautiful figure but also one that is unexpectedly "modern"—in short, the ancient traditional origami figures are simply timeless!

Once you delve into the art of paper folding, however, you will quickly see how multifaceted this seemingly simple activity of paper folding can be. You will also soon recognize the meditative character of origami—a nice way to achieve "balance" in these stressed-out days!

The figures in this book have been specially developed, selected, and arranged to provide pleasure to all—beginners (intentionally, some figures are especially easy to do), intermediates, advanced, and expert. When it seemed advisable, we included in the projects the (sparing) use of scissors; also the use of two sheets of paper for a single figure—no longer considered taboo!

The basic idea of this book is to allow, in fact encourage, young children and adults to come and, yes, "fold" together, enjoying in the process the crafting and creating of an entire origami zoo to add to playtime fun.

I hope that the zoo animals in this book will provide both beginner as well as intermediate paper folders a good start in the art of paper folding, and encourage the more advanced and expert folders—and adult helpers—among you to develop your own original origami figures.

Have fun folding! *Ruth Ungert*

The Art of Paper Folding

Origami for Children

It was discovered some years ago, actually in the middle of the 19th century, that origami was a good group activity for preschoolers. In addition to quiet time and fostering concentration, a child's endeavors were rewarded by the creation of a paper "toy" to play with—and the realization that he or she was able to "do it by myself!"

And don't feel that such younger children can fold only the simplest figures. A number of the more advanced figures presented in this book are quite suitable for this lower-age group. With origami, as with many other activities, it is not age but practice that makes perfect!

Origami offers younger children, in particular, many good opportunities to be actively creative. Although they are at an age in which any talent for drawing is essentially still in the "scribbling phase"—they cannot yet, for example, draw a penguin—with some effort they are able to fold a penguin!

Practice the basic forms with the children in your care and make something creative with them: fold cards, envelopes, and picture frames—there are so many possible uses! Let kites fly and windmills turn. Fold complicated basic shapes out of translucent paper and put them together to make colorful window-mosaics.

Children can learn quite a lot simply by learning to fold; you don't just foster creativity and dexterity with origami! Kids who do origami regularly also learn to follow written and spoken directions

and understand specific definitions, all while engaging in what they see as play. They learn to follow rules as well as to concentrate. Perceptive abilities, thinking, and imagination are also stimulated while children develop a feeling for certain patterns, spatial images, and the relationship of proportions and quantities.

In these fast-moving times, which are very much achievement- and consumer-oriented, it also becomes more and more necessary for children to find peace and to reduce stress. Origami is, of course, no panacea, but it can create a certain sense of balance and a quiet place, while having definite positive effects on self-esteem. Designed especially for younger and preschool children, the folding exercises provided here are simple to do, easy to understand, and a good way to encourage children's budding creative abilities and to confirm them.

Tips for Folding Origami with Children

1. Practice folding each figure that you wish the kids to learn to fold several times yourself. That way you will learn in advance what folding steps may be a problem for them…or for you!

2. Think about whether you might want to simplify a figure for the children, perhaps change it slightly. With many figures, you may decide to simply leave out the final "refining" steps.

3. The kids will need a pleasant and light place to work, and enough sufficiently good materials. Often, inexpensive scrap paper can be used for testing and practicing.

4. Make each fold of the figure step by step along with the children (perhaps using a larger paper) and explain each move in simple words, telling them what to do next.

5. Remember that you will need to show the children your piece of folding in the "right perspective" —theirs.

6. Make sure that the kids understand and carry out each fold in turn. Offer guidance, but do not intrude in their folding unless absolutely necessary.

7. Have the children correct their mistakes themselves, and try to work unsuccessful figures again.

8. Children need a lot of time to think and test things out for themselves, and they enjoy repeating in creative play what they have learned.

9. Praise them a lot, and don't be critical. What does it matter if the children's figures are slightly crooked or wrinkled?

10. Listen to what the children say about the pieces. Everyone's taste is different. Every child should be allowed to determine for themselves what is nice!

11. Many children just can't relate to overly strict or abstract forms. In some cases, a "paper tiger" may be brought to life by simply drawing or sticking on some "eyes." So don't object if the children want to extend their creativity further by decorating their figures.

Tips for Beginners
(especially those who don't wish to stay beginners)

1. In a nice, pleasant spot, set up a work space with a firm, smooth surface. Good lighting is important, too. You need time, a relaxed atmosphere, and peaceful surroundings to do your best paper folding.

2. Don't tackle the hardest figures first. In each section there are easy and more complex folding instructions for various animals in the same group. If you haven't had much experience with origami, start with the exercises at the beginning of the book, then practice the basic (beginner) shapes of those zoo animals you wish to fold. You'll have much more fun creating other figures, once you develop your fingerwork, or dexterity, for folding paper.

3. For your very first folding attempts don't use your most beautiful paper! Keep it safe until you can do your origami well.

4. If you are *really* a beginner, don't start right off folding the zoo animals out of the given size of paper. You can make it easier on yourself by using a larger paper size, for "learning."

5. It is important to make your folds firm, sharp, and as precise as possible. The best way to make most folds is to press down on the center of the new fold with one finger of one hand. Then, adding a single finger from your other hand, smooth the fold down firmly, moving outward from the center in both directions.

6. A fold made in a slightly different place can give the animal a different look or shape, and can sometimes even result in an entirely new figure!

Choosing Your Origami Paper

Origami paper is available in many stationery or arts-and-craft shops. You can choose between simple "folding paper for children" (usually a solid color) and "real origami paper" (which has a white and a colored side). This kind of paper is available in different weights and shades. Particularly nice paper is two-toned or even patterned on one side. Origami paper is offered in small packages sorted in different sizes and often in several color shades and combinations. The quality is often quite varied and it is always worth comparing prices! Square-cut paper exists with edges approximately 4, 6, and 8 inches (10, 15, and 20 cm). These are the most common sizes.

With the exception of the Resting Lions and one of the Elephants, you will be able to fold all figures from origami paper with an edge length of 4 inches (10 cm) and 6 inches (15 cm). You will need a larger starting format for the Resting Lions as well as the Elephant. Furthermore, you will have to cut the paper to size yourself. Of course, you may also cut the paper for the other figures. This is often cheaper and you will be able to fall back upon a larger paper selection. There is, for example, beautiful packing and wrapping paper, the color and structure of which is perfectly suitable for the zoo animals in this book.

Principally, you can use any kind of paper for folding as long as the quality is good enough. If possible, the paper should be thin and tear-resistant. Too soft-fibered paper is not suitable as the folds need to stand out clearly and sharply. With too soft a paper, even the most perfect folds still appear "sloppy" somehow, and the figure tends to cave in easily.

With glazed and colored paper one can fold quite well. Colored paper, however, has the disadvantage that the color at the folds can break easily and the completed figure be, as shown, run through with white lines. Stationery with a maximum weight of 24 pounds can also be used. This paper exists in endless color nuances and it works well with simpler figures that don't have too many folds. Thin, white computer paper is particularly good for practicing. This paper has actually optimal "folding quality." In addition, it is easily available and at a lower price. Computer paper can also be given a quite charming effect—with a little bit of color added. Silhouette paper, which is matted and black on the front and white on the reverse, works great with Penguins and Panda Bears.

Tissue, greaseproof, and transparent paper all work surprisingly well for folding and can be very effective. What is also interesting is that parchment paper, despite its relatively high paper weight, can be quite easily put to use for large-formatted figures. This paper has a marble-like structure and, as shown, can give a quite lovely appearance.

Cutting Your Origami Paper to Size

All the figures in this book are folded from square paper. All four edges must be exactly equal in their length (even to the millimeter!) and must meet at right angles. A figure worked from an unequal square will never work out right! The irregularities will become greater and greater each time the paper is folded to make the figure.

Especially if you have cut the paper to size yourself, you should check before folding to see if it is, indeed, perfectly square. One good way to do this is to make a Shawl Fold as shown and, if necessary, cut off any excess paper.

The paper sizes given for the zoo animals in this book were chosen so that the proportions of the finished folded animals correspond as close as possible to reality. This was done so that the figures would set up well together, side by side, for playing. The largest animal that you will be making is the Giraffe, with an impressive 7 inches (18 cm) of body length. The tiny Duckling, on the other hand, has a body scarcely a half inch (1 cm) in length! Naturally, the folding paper for the Duckling is much smaller than the two pieces of paper used to make the large Giraffe.

Some other animals in this book are also made with two square sheets either placed or glued together after folding. The two pieces of paper may not always be the same size. Often, the paper used to make the head is a bit smaller than the one used for the body. To avoid a lot of figuring and measuring, simply fold the smaller paper inside the body sheet and cut it in the right proportions. Each figure has a folding pattern with a cut showing the paper size required.

Simple Preparation Exercises

Horizontal and Vertical Folds

The Book
1. Fold a rectangular or square paper vertically in the middle. The opposite edges must lie exactly one on top of the other.

2. With many origami figures, another Book Fold is necessary. Open the Book, and repeat the fold in a horizontal direction. The crease lines will cross each other in the middle.

Note: If you leave the Book Fold closed before you do a second Book Fold, you will have a small square made up of four layers of paper on top of each other. It's called the Handkerchief Fold.

The Cupboard
1. Make a Book Fold from a square paper.

2. Open the Book Fold and fold both sides towards the middle line.

3. This is the finished Cupboard.

4. By making even more vertical folds, the paper can be divided into equal strips. (Unfolded, the creases are a good guide to cutting same-size paper strips.)

The Fan
1. Using a rectangular or square piece of paper, fold a Cupboard. Open the cupboard. The three Valley Folds divide the Cupboard into four strips of equal size.

2. Turn the figure over and fold the edges onto the outer lines. This makes two Mountain Folds.

3. Turn the figure over again, and refold the Cupboard.

4. Turn the Cupboard over once more, then fold the edges into the middle line. This results in two Mountain Folds.

5. Fold up the figure. You now a fan made up with eight folds. Mountain and Valley Folds follow, alternating one behind the other (called an Accordion Fold).

Variant: To make a 16-fold fan, turn the Cupboard over

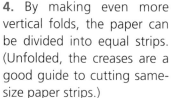

once you have made a total of seven Valley Folds by dividing the strips. Then fold Mountain Folds on the reverse side of the figure, dividing them even more.

The Lattice
1. Make a Cupboard from a square paper. Open up the Cupboard.

2. Repeat the Cupboard, but fold it in a horizontal direction.

3. Open the fold. That is the Lattice. It is made up of 16 equally large squares.

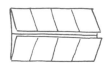

The Lattice is especially well suited as the basis for making houses, boxes, and the simple bodies of animals.

Diagonal Folds

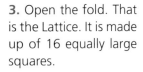

The Shawl Fold
1. Fold a square paper diagonally in the middle. Young children are more likely to do this fold well if it is pointed out to them that the edges of the paper, not only the opposite corners, must lie exactly on top of each other.

2. With many figures, it's necessary that two diagonal folds cross in the middle of the paper. By opening the square sheet of paper completely before folding the second diagonal, you will get a more precise fold.

The Envelope
1. A square paper is used for the Envelope. The white side faces up. Fold the paper on the diagonal middle line.

2. Fold the four corners into the middle.

3. This is the finished Envelope.

The Picture Frame
1. Make an Envelope and open the figure.

2. Fold the four corners toward the inside, on the four outer diagonal lines.

11

3. Now turn the four corners inward.

4. This is the finished Picture Frame.

Heaven and Hell
1. Fold an Envelope.

2. Turn the figure over and fold all four corners into the center again.

3. Turn the figure over and open up the pockets that appear on the reverse side.

4. This form, called Heaven and Hell (because it was often made with blue and red paper), can be used in many different ways and developed further.

5. It is also good to use for making simple hand puppets and animal heads. Simply glue the two opposite inner sides together.

Basic Shapes

The Kite Base

1. A square paper is used for the Kite Base. The white side faces up. Fold the paper together diagonally in the middle.

3. A triangle appears, resulting from the folded sides. Turn the form over.

2. Undo the fold. Then fold both sides along the dashed lines, up to the middle line.

4. This is the finished Kite Base. It's the simplest shape to do and used to make many of the zoo animals in this book. So the animals that begin in this way are better suited for beginners or for the youngest children.

The Fish Base

1. A square paper is used for the Fish Base. Fold the paper as described in steps **1** to **3** of the Kite Base. Then open out the figure.

2. Turn the figure so the creases are at the top. Repeat the Kite Base on the same diagonal, but now folding the form in the opposite direction. Then open out the folds.

3. Press inward along the long creases at the left. At the intersection of the two folds, a small, vertically standing triangle will appear as shown.

4. On the middle line, fold the triangle first upward then downward.

5. Repeat the folds in steps **3** and **4** on the right side of the figure.

6. This is the completed Fish Base.

The Water-Bomb Base

1. A square paper is used for the Water-Bomb Base. The white side faces upward. Fold the paper on the diagonal middle lines.

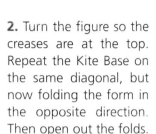

2. Turn the paper over. The colored side now faces up. Fold the paper on the horizontal and vertical middle lines.

3. Fold the paper under along the middle horizontal line so that a triangle with two inside lying wings arises.

4. This is the finished Water-Bomb Base.

The Windmill Base

1. A square paper is used for the Windmill. The white side faces up. Fold the paper the same way you did to make the Envelope and the Lattice.

2. Pull the sides and the corners of the figure upward by placing the double triangles at each of the small corners of the diagonals on top of each other.

3. Fold the lower and the upper edges onto the horizontal middle line so that both the

right and the left edges lie along the vertical middle line at the same time.

4. Fold the left lower wing to the right and the right upper wing to the left. This is the finished Windmill.

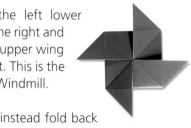

5. If you instead fold back the right lower wing to the left and the left upper wing to the right, you will get a Windmill that turns in the opposite direction.

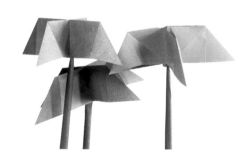

The Bird Base

1. A square paper is used for the Bird Base. The colored side faces up. Fold the paper at the diagonal middle folds.

2. Turn the paper over. The white side now faces up. Fold the paper on the horizontal and vertical middle line to make creases.

3. Fold the paper together along the middle line so make a smaller square with two inside-lying wings.

4. With the open side of the figure pointing downward, fold the two wings of the top layer along the middle line.

5. Fold the triangle on the dashed line downward. Press this fold firmly.

6. Undo the folds of steps **4** and **5** folds.

7. Carefully open the front part of the figure by pulling the lower corner of the top layer upward as far as possible.

8. This will form a diamond shape. Press the figure flat. The open wings point downward.

9. Turn the figure over and repeat steps **4** to **8** on the reverse side of the figure.

10. This is the finished Bird Base. Two open, narrow points lie next to each other at the bottom. At the top, two closed, wide points are positioned on top of each other; in-between you have a small triangle.

Basic Folding Techniques and Terms

Mountain Fold

Before the fold, the white (inner) side of the paper faces upward. Fold it into a Book. Unfold and turn the paper over. The fold points upward.

Valley Fold
Before the fold, the colored (outer) side of the paper faces upward. Fold the paper into a Book. Unfold. The outer side fold points downward.

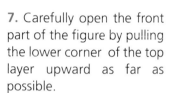

Accordion Fold
A series of Mountain and Valley Folds that follow
each other in an alternating way produces an Accordion Fold. To make the folds, it is necessary to turn the paper before each new fold. An Accordion Fold is then turned into a Fan by making a Book Fold of the paper. With a diagonal fold, you will get triangular patterns.

Tip: The constant turning of the paper back and forth to make a Fan, with its many folds, can quickly become annoying. Also, the folds tend to become irregular. Look on page 10 to see how you can easily make a Fan with equal folds.

Inside Crimp Fold

Open up a diagonally folded paper. Make an Accordion Fold (first a Mountain Fold and then a Valley Fold) with one corner of the paper. Fold the paper together diagonally again. Hold the lower edge of the figure firmly and carefully pull the small point upward. On the inside of the figure, as shown, you will get another "soft" fold. The small tip is pointed in an obtuse, or wide, angle, away from the bend. By firmly pressing on the outer side of the form, you can strengthen this Inside Crimp Fold.

Outside Crimp Fold

Again, open up a diagonally folded paper. On one corner of the paper, make an Accordion Fold (first a Valley Fold and then a Mountain Fold). Fold the paper together diagonally once more. Then, while holding the lower edge of the figure steady, carefully pull the small point upward. On the outer side of the figure, as shown, you will get a "soft" fold. The small point now points away from the bend, again in an obtuse angle. By firmly pressing on the outside, you can strengthen this Outside Crimp Fold.

Reverse Fold

With a diagonally folded paper, prefold a corner diagonally backward. Undo the fold and allow the figure to open slightly. At the upper part of the creased figure, you will see on the right of the diagonal crease a Mountain Fold and on the left of the diagonal crease a Valley Fold. Press your finger along this outer edge of the Mountain Fold and slightly over the crossing point of the three creases. The right side of the figure now turns slightly backward (inside out). Slowly and carefully fold the figure together diago-

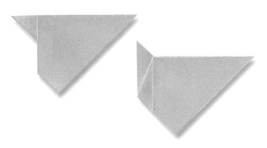

nally again, without letting go of the crossing point. In this way, the left side of the point will turn backward (inside out) also. Again, fold the form together diagonally and press the fold flat. The Mountain Fold has turned into a Valley Fold, and you've made a Reverse Fold.

Sink Fold

With the paper folded diagonally, prefold a corner diagonally downward. Undo the corner fold again. Allow the figure to open slightly. On the outer side, there is to the right of the center crease a Mountain Fold and to the left of that crease a Valley Fold. Push the diagonal crease at the top of the form inward from top to the side creases, and at the same time fold the figure together diagonally again. Press the fold flat firmly from the outside. The Valley Fold has turned into a Mountain fold; and you've made a Sink Fold.

Squash Fold

With the paper folded diagonally, prefold a corner diagonally downward and undo the fold. Keeping the lower part of the figure closed, open the prefolded corner out to the sides and press downward on it until it rests right on the diagonal fold. Push down on the Kite shape that appears until it lies against the front side of the figure—it's a Squash Fold.

My Colorful Origami Zoo

Welcome to the colorful origami zoo! It's a lot of fun to set up an entire zoo—with many animals in their habitats. But it's also a lot of work, because almost everything in this origami zoo must be folded: each of the animals in the zoo and the bushes and trees. The meadows can be made from large sheets of green paper or some fabric.

A long blue silk scarf can become a body of water, and a small mirror a frozen pond. "Water" can also be cut to size from blue-tinted cardboard and wrapped in a bit of plastic wrap to give it a shiny water effect.

A few nice stones, shells, and pieces of bark picked up from outdoors and cleaned up can add to your colorful zoo. You may even have some items in your own home that can be used for your origami zoo. Small carton boxes can become houses or caves for the animals. Maybe you will want to use a cooling rack to help control the wildest of your zoo animals.

Behind this zoo there is a Duck Pond...so, please turn the page and come right ahead!

At the Duck Pond

They seem to be having a grand time at the Duck Pond: There, Mother Ducks splash around with their Ducklings, quacking in competition with the Frogs! Some of the Frogs are sunning themselves on flat rocks, in the shelter of reed grass and bushes. Have you already found the small green croakers?

Ducklings * * *

Basic Shape: Kite Base
Paper: Two-color origami paper,
     e.g., yellow/red
Cutting: 6"   15 cm

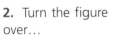

1. Make a Kite Base. If you want the Duckling to have a different colored bill, first fold a small corner backwards.

2. Turn the figure over…

3. …and fold the upper point downward.

4. Turn the point upward one more time.

5. Fold the figure together in the middle. Then, as shown by the dashed line,…

6. …form the neck with a Reverse Fold. On the dashed line…

7. …form the head with a Reverse Fold. Then, following the dashed lines,…

8. …form the bill with an Accordion Fold.

9. Carefully, pull the Duckling's tail in an upward direction and firmly press the new fold (Crimp Fold) together. Then, as shown by the dashed line,…

10. …fold the two lower edges toward the inside.

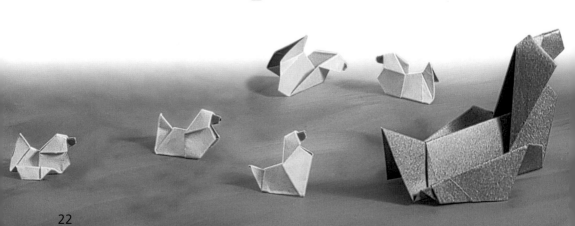

22

Mama Duck * * *

Basic Shape: Kite Base
Paper: Two-color origami paper,
e.g., brown/red
Cutting: 6″ 15 cm

1. For Mama Duck, follow the instructions for the Duckling figure from folding steps **1** through **5**. Then, on the dashed line,…

2. …form the neck with a Reverse Fold. Following the dashed line,…

3. …the head is then formed with a Reverse Fold. At the head, pull the Reverse Fold slightly in an upward direction and firmly press the new fold. On the dashed lines…

4. …form the bill with an Accordion Fold and pull slightly downward. The Duck's tail is pulled in an upward direction. Fold the two lower edges of the figure upward.

5. On the dashed lines…

6. …fold the two wings downward again.

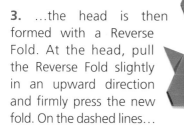

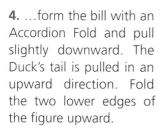

Jumping Frog *

Basic Shape: Water-Bomb Base
Paper: Two-color origami paper,
e.g., light green/dark green
Cutting: 4″ 10 cm

1. Make a Water-Bomb Base.

2. Open the figure and then fold two corners toward the center.

3. Undo the last step and return once more to the shape of the Water-Bomb Base.

4. Turn the figure over and fold the Frog's legs toward the middle line. On the dashed line…

5. …fold the two legs outward once again.

6. Turn the Frog over. If, shortly and firmly with your fingertip, you tap the very outer point of the rear of the Frog's head, the Frog will jump into the air!

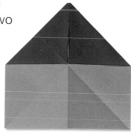

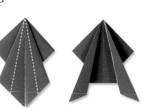

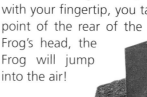

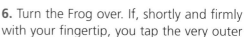

Bull Frog * *

Basic Shape: Water-Bomb Base
Paper: Two-color origami paper,
     e.g., green/orange
Cutting: 4" | 10 cm

1. Make a Water-Bomb Base

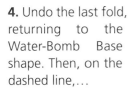

2. Fold the two points in the front onto the middle line; first in an upward direction…

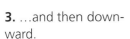

3. …and then downward.

4. Undo the last fold, returning to the Water-Bomb Base shape. Then, on the dashed line,…

5. …prefold and open the front part of the figure. Place the two large triangles on top of each other and firmly press the front part of the figure upward.

6. Fold the small triangles so that the inside of the paper becomes visible.

7. Press the triangles together along the creased lines so that the frog's eyes are standing vertically.

8. The legs of the bullfrog are folded in the same way as described in steps **4** and **5** of the frog.

Blades of Grass * *

Basic Shape: Kite Base
Paper: Origami paper,
     e.g., light green
Cutting: 6" | 15 cm

1. Make a Kite Base.

2. Repeat the folds of the Kite Base in opposite directions.

3. Fold the two points on top of each other.

4. Fold the figure together in the middle.

5. Pull the point that is on the inside slightly toward the outside and firmly press the fold that appears at the bottom of the figure.

Lawn or Marsh Grasses *

Basic Shape: Book Base
Paper: Origami paper, e.g., light green
Cutting: 6″  15 cm

4. Fold the figure together again and crease the Book as often as you like into an Accordion shape.

1. Make a Book Base.

2. Fold over the bend in an upward direction.

3. Open the figure, press the middle bend flat, then change the Valley Fold on the reverse of the figure into a Mountain Fold.

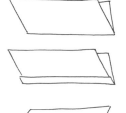

5. Cut into the paper from the edges to make different blades or shapes of grass.

6. Open up the cut fold and bring the figure together as described in step **3**.

The Lions' Den

Now we are coming to the Lions' Den. In the shadow of the trees, old Pasha quietly rests with his Lion friends. But Little Lion seems quite excited! His friend, Little Tiger, has just arrived for a visit with Mama Tiger (who is folded the same way as the Resting Lions).

Little Lion * *

Basic Shapes: Fish Base, Shawl Fold
Paper: Origami paper, e.g., light brown,
and dark brown (optional for mane)
Cutting: 4"

10 cm

1. For the body, make a Fish Base using light brown.

2. Open the figure and fold the two small corners inward.

3. Return the figure to the Fish Base shape.

4. Fold the figure together in the middle. Then, on the dashed line,…

5. …make a Sink Fold. Push this fold down from top to bottom so that the Lion's tail stands up vertically.

6. With a Sink Fold, prefold the tuft of the tail, then fold it back into a diamond shape. This is the body of the Lion cub.

7. For the head, use a diagonally folded piece of matching paper. The colored side faces up.

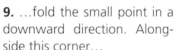

8. Fold the two points along the edges downward. On the dashed line…

9. …fold the small point in a downward direction. Alongside this corner…

10. …fold the two small corners upward again.

11. Turn the figure over. Then, on the dashed lines,…

12. …fold the corners upward so that the nose of the Lion appears. The tips of the ears are slightly folded inward. That is the Lion's head.

13. Glue the head to the body at any angle you wish. Do you want the Lion cub to be a little older, already have a mane? If you do, you can make a fold-cut as described for "Wild Lion."

And His Friend, Little Tiger * *

Basic Shapes: Fish Base, Shawl Fold
Paper: Two-color origami paper,
  e.g., brown and orange stripes / white
Cutting: 4"

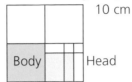

10 cm

Body | Head

1. As is the case with his friend the Little Lion, the body of the Little Tiger begins with a Fish Base. If you are not able to find appropriately striped paper, diagonally running stripes can be drawn with a felt pen onto both sheets (body and head) of your "tiger paper" before you fold the base. Open out the Fish Base and fold the small corners outward.

2. Return your figure to the folds of the Fish Base. The Little Tiger now has white paws. Turn the figure over.

3. On the dashed line…

4. …prefold the tail. Then fold it together along the line as shown, somewhat similar to the Accordion Fold. Next…

5. …fold the tip of the tail in an upward direction. Press the two little triangles of the tip of the tail together slightly so that the tip stands out backward a little bit.

6. The head of the Little Tiger is folded in exactly the same way as the head of the Little Lion; there are only two slight differences: on the dashed line for the "nose fold," the corner on the bottom is folded inward and the pointed ears stay as they are. The Mama of the Little Tiger is folded in exactly the same as the Resting Lion.

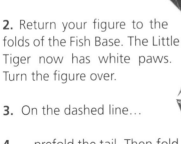

Wild Lion * *

Basic Shapes: Heaven and Hell, Windmill Base
Paper: Origami paper, e.g., light brown, and dark brown
Cutting:

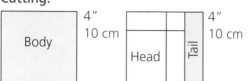

1. For the head, fold your light brown paper into the Heaven and Hell shape. Divide the two marked triangles in half by gluing them together along the vertical middle line. Now you have a kind of finger puppet with a movable creased mouth. Turn the figure over.

2. On the dashed lines…

3. …fold the two bottom corners inward and the two top corners outward. To make the round ears of the Lion, fold the corners back again.

4. For the body, make a Windmill fold up to step **3.**

5. Fold the two right wings to the left side and, on the dashed lines…

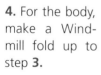

6. …fold these two wings inward. These are the front legs of the Lion. Now, along the dashed lines…

7. …fold the hind legs outward.

8. Fold the lion's body together in the middle.

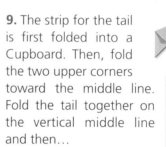

9. The strip for the tail is first folded into a Cupboard. Then, fold the two upper corners toward the middle line. Fold the tail together on the vertical middle line and then…

10. …glue it into the bend of the lion's body. Note that a small piece of it still has to stick out in the front because the Lion's head will need to be attached to it. Glue this little piece against the back of the lower "middle wall" of the head. On the other end, you can get the tail "twitching" with two reverse folds on the dashed lines.

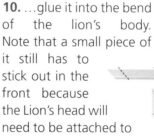

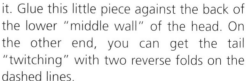

11. The Lion's mane is made from a fold-cut. Open the Lion's mane…

12. …and cut into it up to one of the center lines. Fold two strips outward to glue the mane to the body.

13. Attach the lower half of the strips to the front of the lion's body. The head of the lion, as shown, will be movable and the openings on the back of the head are completely covered by the mane.

Resting Lions * * *

Basic Shapes: Kite Base
Paper: Origami paper, e.g., light brown
Cutting: 8″ □ 20 cm
(2 pieces)

Old Lion
1. Make a Kite Base. Following the dashed lines…

2. …fold both sides toward the middle line.

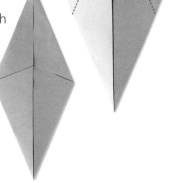

3. Turn the figure over. Fold the figure in the middle and turn it over again. Along the dashed line…

4. …bring the top point toward the bottom.

5. Fold the figure together in the middle.

6. Pull the right point far enough upward so a piece of what will be the Lion's paws can still be seen. On the dashed line…

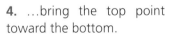

7. …make a Sink Fold. Undo the Sink Fold again and, along the dashed line,…

8. …Sink Fold the point inward. Then return to the Sink Fold and, on the dashed line…

9. …make a small Squash Fold to form ears on both sides of the Lion figure. Do a Sink Fold…

10. …on the dashed line. Make the Lion's tail narrower…

11. …on both sides of the figure. On the dashed line…

12. …fold the tail upward using a Sink Fold. Then, at the tip of the tail, make another Sink Fold…

13. …on the dashed line and open the fold outward so that a diamond-shaped tuft appears at the end of the tail. This is the Old Lion.

Younger Lion

14. The Younger Lion is folded in exactly the same way as the older one up to and including step **6.** Then, on the dashed lines…

15. …make two Reverse Folds. On this next dashed line…

16. …fold the point inward. Then, on the dashed line…

17. …fold the corners of both sides of the figure outward. Form the tail of the Young Lion just as described with the Old Lion.

Bush and Tree *

Basic Shape: Cupboard
Paper: Origami paper, e.g., marbled yellow-green and dark brown

Cutting: 6″   15 cm
(3 pieces)

Bush
Treetop
Trunk

Bush

1. Make a Cupboard.

2. Fold the Cupboard together in the middle, top to bottom, as shown in the second illustration so that the folds are on the inside. On the dashed lines at the top of the bend, make the prefold for two Sink Folds.

3. Open the figure and fold all four side corners inward slightly diagonally as shown.

4. Close the figure while you push the Sink Folds inward. This is the finished Bush. To make bushes of different heights, fold the lower edges inward as high as you like. To make a group of bushes or an entire hedge, put several of these bushes together, overlapping them slightly, and perhaps glue them together.

Tree

5. You may also use the Bush as the crown of a Tree. For the trunk, make a Cupboard, using the brown paper. Cut it along the vertical middle line into two parts.

6. Once separated, fold each strip once again into a Cupboard, then fold each of the figures in half vertically, right down the middle. Shorten the two trunks to the desired height.

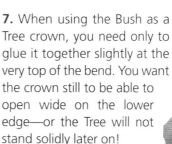

7. When using the Bush as a Tree crown, you need only to glue it together slightly at the very top of the bend. You want the crown still to be able to open wide on the lower edge—or the Tree will not stand solidly later on!

8. Glue only one end of the tree trunk onto only one lower edge of the crown on the inside. Spread the base of the trunk slightly to set up the Tree.

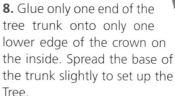

With the Penguins

Here lives an entire Penguin colony. Penguins are very polite and sociable. They even get along with the dangerous Polar Bears. But the small Polar Bear looks a bit unhappy. Maybe he is feeling cold?

Papa Penguin **

Basic Shape: Fish Base
Paper: Two-color origami paper,
e.g., black/white
Cutting: 6"   15 cm

1. Make the Fish Base but do it a little differently, so the edges aren't all lying right along the middle line. Then, following the dashed line,…

2. …make an Inside Crimp Fold to form the beak. Then, make an Accordion Fold right under the tip of the wing.

3. Fold the figure together in the middle. On the dashed line…

4. …form the head with a Reverse Fold. Pull the point of the beak slightly lower. To form the feet, make a cut on the crease, at the lower point of the form, from the bottom up to the belly.

5. First, fold the two cut foot sections upward and then to the front, as shown, so that the soles of the feet will stand flat on the ground. This is Papa Penguin.

Mama Penguin ***

Basic Shape: Fish Base
Paper: Two-color origami paper,
e.g., black/white
Cutting: 6"   15 cm

1. The Fish Base and the Accordion Fold of the beak tip are creased the same for Mama Penguin as for Papa Penguin. Fold the figure together in the

middle and, on the dashed line…

2. …fold the point into a backward Sink Fold. Then, on the dashed line,…

3. …the point of the foot is brought back to the front with another Sink Fold and the head is shaped with a Reverse Fold. Push the tips of the feet a little to flatten them.

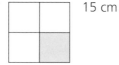
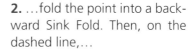

Baby Penguin *

Basic Shape: Kite Base
Paper: Two-color origami paper,
e.g., black/white
Cutting: 6" 15 cm

1. Make the Kite Base in a way so, again, the edges don't lie exactly along the middle line.

2. Open the figure and fold the right and left corners to the inside.

3. Close the figure and, at the point, make an Inside Accordion Fold for the beak.

4. Fold the figure together in the middle and along the dashed lines…

5. …form the head with a Reverse Fold, and the tail with a Sink Fold. Along the dashed line…

6. …fold the stomach on both sides of the figure with two Sink Folds, extending a little to the inside. For a rounder baby's beak, you may fold the point of the beak slightly toward the inside. Finally, pull the end of the beak downward a little bit.

Tip: If you would like to make Polar Bears for a scene in addition to your Penguins, turn to and follow the directions for making Bears, but just use white paper instead.

With the Giraffes

Our next stop is the Giraffes. What beautiful but strange creatures they are—with their long necks. But they certainly do need them! How else would they be able to reach those tender leaves high up in the trees? The Baby Giraffe, however, seems so young. Look, it is even having a hard time trying to stand upright on its wobbly little legs.

Giraffe ★★★

Basic Shape: Fish Base
Paper: Origami paper, e.g., marbled yellow
Cutting: 6″   15 cm
(2 pieces)

1. Make two Fish Base shapes. To form the head and neck of the Giraffe out of one form, fold the small wings back in an upward direction. Turn the figure over and, along the dashed line,…

2. …fold the two upper edges to the middle line.

3. Now, fold the figure together along the middle line, and bring the small wings downward. On the dashed line…

4. …form the Giraffe's head with a Reverse Fold. Then, following the dashed line,…

5. …fold the head point back with a Reverse Fold. Bring the ears upward and then, on the dashed line,…

6. …fold the Giraffe's mane. The ears are again folded downward and slightly opened. Cut into the point for the horns up to the back of the head, and fold the horns outward. Again, following the dashed line…

7. …make a Sink Fold. Fold the leftover point inward as shown so that it disappears entirely into the Giraffe's neck.

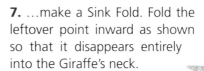

8. For the Giraffe's body, the Fish Base is folded together so that both small wings are on the outside. On the dashed line…

9. …fold the hind legs of the Giraffe with a Sink Fold. Fold both wings back and then, as shown by the dashed line,…

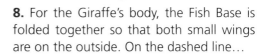

10. …form the forelegs with a Sink Fold.

11. Bring the Sink Fold of the forelegs back and outward.

12. Now, fold the wings forward and then fold the points of the legs slightly inward. This way the Giraffe can stand freely. Cut into the legs

along the bend, and push the four legs slightly outward.

13. Now, put the head section into the body. Insert the neck in a straight line to the forelegs and the Giraffe will stand very securely. Because of the somewhat longer forelegs, it is well balanced despite being top-heavy.

Glue the head and the body together and, at the same time, fold the wings on the body around the Giraffe's neck.

Baby Giraffe ★★★★

Basic Form: Bird Base
Paper: Origami paper, e.g., marbled yellow
Cutting: 6″ 15 cm

1. Make a Bird Base. Turn the figure like this, so that the open points lie on top. On the dashed line…

2. …fold both sides to the middle line. Turn the figure over, and repeat this fold on the reverse side. On the dashed line…

3. …fold the left wing of the figure downward. To do that you need to first open the left wing and, after making the fold, close it again. Then, on the dashed line…

4. …form the Giraffe's neck with a Sink Fold. On the dashed line, fold and unfold the triangle on the back of the Giraffe on both sides of the figure. Pull the hind leg a little to the right. Seen from above, a small diamond now appears on the back. Following the dashed line…

5. …form the Giraffe's head with a Reverse Fold. Fold the tip of the nose inward. Fold the corners on the back side of the head downward on both sides of the figure as ears. On the dashed line, fold both forelegs slightly outward so that the Giraffe's front legs go into a light split.

6. The Baby Giraffe stands very well on its three legs. But if you'd prefer four legs, just cut into the hind legs along the center crease to make one more.

A Giraffe from Strips *

Basic Form: Fan
Paper: Origami paper, e.g., yellow
Cutting: 6"   15 cm

1. Fold an eight-section Fan, and cut the Fan on every other fold, into a total of four doubled strips. Open one of the strips.

2. On one of the folded strips, make a Reverse Fold, as shown by the dashed line. This forms the head of the giraffe. Then fold the three other strips together in the middle.

3. Now, open the three strips completely. Form two strips into legs by making little inward folds on all four of the corners. On the body strip, fold only the two corners inward.

4. Fold the strips for the legs together again, and make a Sink Fold on the head.

5. Firmly paste the legs and head piece on one half of the body strip.

6. Before you paste down the other half of the body strip, you can slightly fold out one corner as a small tail again or stick on a mane for the Giraffe. Ears and horns can be additionally attached, or you can fold back both corners on the back of the head as ears.

Bush and Tree **

Basic Shape: Water-Bomb Base, Kite Base
Paper: Origami paper, e.g., green and brown
Cutting: 6" / 15 cm
(three pieces)

Bush

1. Make a Water-Bomb Base.

2. Open the Water-Bomb Base and fold all four corners slightly inward.

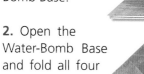

3. Next, fold the figure back into the shape of the Water-Bomb Base. On the dashed lines…

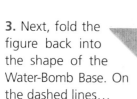

4. …make Sink Folds on all four wings of the figure. Fold the wings to the side so that they point in all four directions. This is the finished Bush.

5. If you prefer a more closed shape Bush, you can add some glue to the wings on the inside, to stick them together. Then the Bush will not open so wide anymore.

Tree

6. You can also use the Bush as the crown of a Tree. Using brown paper, make a Kite Base for the trunk. Then, on the dashed lines…

7. …fold both sides to the middle line once more.

8. Fold the figure together in the middle as shown, so that the folds lie on the inside. Now, follow the dashed line…

9. …and make a Reverse Fold. Place or glue the crown on the trunk so that the Tree is in balance.

At the Elephant House

Look, we've found the Elephants! Not just one but several small Elephants can be seen here under the palm trees. Old Father Elephant is nearby watching over his children.

Sitting Elephant **

Basic Shape: Kite Base
Paper: Origami paper, e.g., gray
Cutting: 6" 15 cm

1. Make a Kite Base.

2. Fold the figure together in the middle. Along the dashed line…

3. …do a Reverse Fold. Do another Reverse Fold as shown by the dashed line and…

4. …you will form the back of the Elephant's head. Now, along the dashed line…

5. …fold the trunk downward with a Sink Fold. Make another Sink Fold on the dashed line…

6. …to move the trunk upward again. Give the trunk its final shape with two Reverse Folds.

7. Now, on the dashed line, make a Sink Fold for the tail and, on the dashed line on both sides of the figure,…

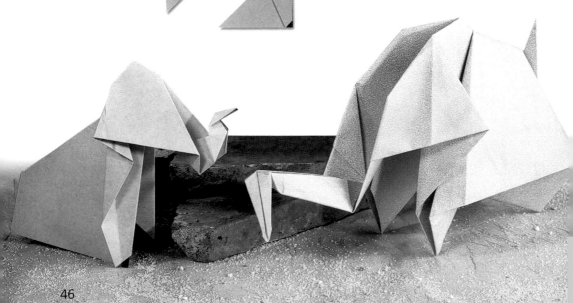

8. …fold the legs and ears forward. Again, undo the folds and…

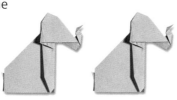

9. …pull the tip of the tail upward. Fix it in position with a Crimp Fold, and also adjust the folds of the ears. Depending on how you like the position of the ears and forelegs and the angle of the Elephant's head, there are many possibilities.

Standing Elephant **

Basic Shape: Kite Base
Paper: Origami paper, e.g., gray
Cutting: 14"   35 cm
(approx.)

1. This Elephant is folded just like the Resting Lions up to and including step **7**. Then the figure is merely turned so that what is the Lion's nose there becomes the hind leg of the Elephant here. Along the dashed line…

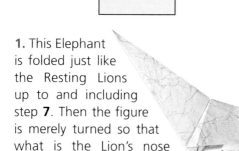

2. …make a Sink Fold, and pull the tip of the tail slightly upward. On the dashed line…

3. …lay out the position of the head and the trunk with a Sink Fold.

4. Fold the ears to the side on both sides of the figure.

5. Bring the ears backward again and firmly press them for a Squash Fold. Open the trunk out…

6. …into a diamond, and fold it as shown making the lower part narrower.

7. Fold the trunk together again. On the dashed line…

8. …form the trunk, shaping it with two Sink Folds.

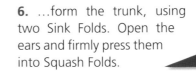

Baby Elephant ★★★★

Basic Shape: Fish Base, Windmill Base
Paper: Two-color origami paper,
        e.g., blue/white
Cutting: 6″ ⬜ 15 cm
(2 pieces)

1. For the head, make a Fish Base. The two tips should point downward. Turn the figure over and, on the dashed lines,…

2. …fold both sides to the middle line. Again, following the dashed lines,…

3. …make an Accordion Fold. Fold the figure together as shown along the middle line…

4. …so that the sections for the ears lie on top. Pull the trunk upward a bit and, on the dashed line, bring the trunk upward again with a Sink Fold. Fold the ears forward and, on the other dashed line,…

5. …make a Reverse Fold. Fold the lower point, the neck, back along the dashed line with a Reverse Fold. On both other dashed lines…

6. …form the trunk, using two Sink Folds. Open the ears and firmly press them into Squash Folds.

7. For the body, make a Windmill Base up to step number **3**.

8. Fold the figure in the middle as shown, so that the open sides lie on the outside. Fold all four wings of the Windmill inward half way, and open the prefolds again.

9. Firmly press all four wings into Squash Folds.

10. Open up the figure, and make an Accordion Fold along the dashed lines.

11. Fold the figure together again and pull the left side downward slightly. Press the Crimp Fold down firmly. The toes of the Elephant come from the Accordion Folds made on the dashed lines.

12. Glue or paste the head piece onto the body as shown so that the end of the back point is seen as only a little tail.

Sitting Elephant Baby ★★★★

Basic Shape: Fish Base
Paper: Origami paper, e.g., gray
Cutting: 6″ — 15 cm

1. Make a Fish Base. The two tips point upward. Turn the figure over and, on the dashed lines,…

2. …fold both sides in toward the middle. For the head, make an Accordion Fold on the dashed lines.

3. Then turn the figure over and fold both tips outward for the ears.

4. Fold the figure together along the middle line so that the ears lie inward. On the dashed lines…

5. …make Sink Folds. At the head Accordion Fold, pull the trunk upward slightly. On the three dashed lines…

6. …make a Sink Fold for the foot and the trunk. Then, on the dashed line,…

7. …fold the body of the Elephant downward on both sides of the figure. The ears are opened and pressed firmly as a Squash Fold.

Elephant ★★★★

Basic Shape: Bird Base
Paper: Two-color origami paper,
     e.g., gray/white
Cutting: 6″   15 cm
(2 pieces)

1. Make two Bird
Bases.

2. On the Bird Base for the Elephant head, fold one of the narrow, open points together in the middle. This point comes up later as the tusks. On the dashed line…

3. …bring the other open point downward with a Reverse Fold. That is the Elephant's trunk.

4. Open the point of the tusks, and cut into it along the dashed line.

5. Fold the cut point back as shown so that the trunk lies between both parts of the tusk. On the dashed line…

6. …fold the tusks downward with a Reverse Fold so that

the white side of the paper faces up. On the dashed line…

7. …the tusks are brought upward again with a Sink Fold. Place the lower open side of the trunk over the starting point of the tusks. On the dashed line…

8. …both ears are folded forward, and again on the dashed line…

9. …fold the ears back and lay them in folds as shown; the ears should stand out a little bit. Later, the outer corner on the back side of the head will be glued against the Elephant's body.

10. Again, open the Bird Base to form the body and toes of the Elephant. At each one of the four corners, make a small Accordion Fold.

11. Fold the Bird Base together as shown so that all four wings are underneath and the Elephant's legs point forward and backward in pairs.

12. Glue the corner of the back of the head right above the forelegs. If the Elephant, after standing for a long period of time, tends to "stretch out on all fours," you can improve its posture again by gluing together two parts inside at the very top of the bend.

Palm Tree **

Basic Shape: Windmill Base
Paper: Origami paper, e.g., green and brown
Size: 6"   15 cm
(2 pieces)

1. Make a Windmill Base up to step **3.**

2. Turn the figure over. Fold a "sink point" by putting together the square in the middle of the Windmill Base as shown, as if folding a Water-Bomb Base.

3. On the dashed line, fold a forward and a rear point to each side. Turn the figure over.

4. This is how the Windmill Base looks now from up above. Secure the Water-Bomb Base with a little glue so the figure won't spring open.

5. For the trunk, tightly roll a piece of paper diagonally and secure it with a little glue. The trunk's shape should be slightly wider as it goes down toward the ground.

6. Flatten the narrower tip of the trunk, add glue to hold, and position it into a wing from below as close as possible to the middle point of the Windmill Base.

Tip: For use as a decoration, place the foot of the Palm Tree in a small container of sand, the holes of a brick, or a small lump of clay.

In the Reptile House

In the Reptile House, there is a gigantic Crocodile that is almost as big as a dragon, some Turtles, and dangerous Boa Constrictors.

Lizard *

Basic Shape: Fish Base
Paper: Origami paper, e.g., green
Size: 6"   15 cm

1. Make a Fish Base. Both tips point upward.

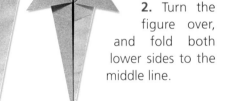

2. Turn the figure over, and fold both lower sides to the middle line.

3. Turn the figure over again, and fold both wings as widely as possible diagonally outward as legs.

4. Fold both legs halfway up again.

5. Fold the figure together along the middle line so that the legs lie on top. On the dashed line, make the prefold for a Squash Fold.

6. Open the left corner of the figure from underneath, and firmly press the Squash Fold toward the right. Make as many Accordion Folds as you want on the tail of the Lizard.

Crocodile ****

Basic Form: Bird Base, Kite Base
Paper: Two-color origami paper,
          e.g., red/green
Size:

Body	4" 10 cm	Head	4" 10 cm

1. For the head of the Crocodile, make a Bird Base up to step **8**. On the dashed lines…

2. …fold the paper of the inner side outward. In order to do so, open the diamond, and then fold. Begin at the points and fold in the direction of the

middle bend only as far as the tension of the paper allows.

3. When you snap the diamond into the Crocodile's mouth at the middle bend and firmly press the edges, the missing remainder of the fold will appear by itself.

4. Turn the figure over and, on the reverse side, fold on the dashed lines.

5. Open the Crocodile's eyes with two Squash Folds and set the eyes perpendicularly.

6. For the body, fold a Kite Base, except that the edges should not entirely line up with the diagonal bend. On the dashed lines…

7. …fold both upper edges of the figure downward.

8. Fold the figure together in a horizontal direction any number of times, like a Fan. Both end points can jut out a good way.

9. Open the Fan and close the figure together in the middle. Do the preliminary fold for a Sink Fold on each second fold.

10. Open the figure slightly from below. Now it becomes really tricky! Fold the figure together once more little by little to form a Fan and, at the same time, push half of each Sink Fold toward the bottom. Did it work for you? If so, you have earned the title "Origami Professional!" The Crocodile body is the most difficult figure in this book to do.

11. Glue the head to the body as shown so that the Crocodile does not become top-heavy.

Boa Constrictor *

Basic Shape: Fan Base
Paper: Two-color origami paper,
        e.g., orange/green
Size: 6"   15 cm

1. The Boa Constrictor consists of a 16-fold Fan folded in a diagonal direction. For a consistent fold, you must fold the paper twice diagonally first. At the beginning, the side with the color lies upward, but later it becomes the color of the snake's stomach.

2. When you make the folds, you can do them the same way as given for making a Fan from a Cupboard (on page 10). For a diagonally folded Fan, the only difference is that it's not the edges of the paper but rather the corners of the paper that are laid one on top of the other!

3. After the preliminary folds, make a total of seven Valley Folds and eight Mountain Folds into a diagonal Fan. Then, following the dashed lines…

4. …make two Reverse Folds for the head and one Reverse Fold for the tail. As shown, fold…

5. …the tip of the tail backward on both sides of the figure. Flatten the head of the Boa Constrictor slightly by pushing it down from above. On the dashed lines…

6. …fold the body of the snake into Accordion Folds.

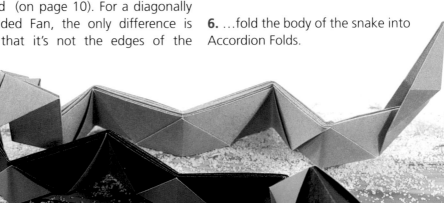

Turtle ✳✳✳

Basic Shape: Windmill Base
Paper: Two-color origami paper,
    e.g., gray bamboo pattern/white
Size: 6"   15 cm

1. Make a Windmill Base up to step **3.** Sink the middle point of the Windmill Base, as described with the Palm Tree.

2. Fold half of all four Windmill wings upward, then fold the four wings back again.

3. Open the figure entirely and make a Reverse Fold on each edge along the preliminary fold of step **2.** Again, close the figure into the sunken Windmill.

4. Push from underneath, as shown, on the center of the figure, so the shape folds up and outward.

You should now have a kind of shell shape with four feet.

5. Open the figure on one side and pull this side out so that the paper can lie doubled along the middle line. The point that arises here becomes the head of the Turtle. Hold the head in this position, and close the shell of the Turtle. In that way, folds appear on both sides of the head and prevent the head from refolding. Press this kind of Crimp Fold firmly from the outside.

6. Fold down a small corner at the back of the shell. Open this preliminary fold and press the small "double-triangle" that appears inward, as a Sink Fold. Make small Sink Folds on both lateral corners of the Turtle's shell, too.

With the Bears

Mother Bear would like to be relaxing and lazy, but she has two extremely lively cubs to take care of! Where do you suppose the larger of the two cubs might be? Mama growls, and here comes the young Bear, running as fast as he can. He was probably over visiting the two Pandas.

Mother Bear **

Basic Shape: Windmill Base, Shawl Fold
Paper: Two-color origami paper,
        e.g., light brown/dark brown
Size:

Body	6" 15 cm		6" 15 cm
			Head

1. For Mother Bear, shape the body as you did the Wild Lion, and make a small Sink Fold on the back.

2. Fold the paper for the head of Mother Bear diagonally in the middle twice. Fold and unfold the paper on both dashed lines.

3. Fold in the right and left corners up to the creases, and close the figure in the middle.

4. For the ears, bring the corners down on the dashed lines, and turn the corner upward for the nose.

5. Open the ears into Squash Folds, but don't press them entirely flat. Bend the ears slightly forward. Bring the triangled back of the snout forward as shown so that it is not completely hidden by the front part. Fold both halves of the head slightly rearward along the bridge of the nose so that the head becomes more pliant. Glue the back of the head, at any angle you wish, to one side of the Bear's body. At the same time, make sure that the Bear's head is not pressed flat again!

Bear Cub **

Basic Shape: Shawl Fold, Water-Bomb Base
Paper: Two-color origami paper,
        e.g., light brown/dark brown
Size: 6"

		15 cm
	Body	
		Head

1. The head is folded in a similar way to that of the Mother Bear. In proportion to the larger paper and body format, small folding differences will make the head of the cub seem rounder and more childlike.

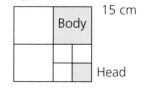

Fold the diagonally prefolded paper for the head without the nose folds of the Mother Bear. Both corners are simply folded inward up to the middle line. Fold the figure together in the middle.

2. Continue, then, just as described with the head of the Mother Bear.

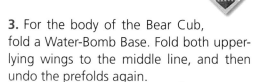

3. For the body of the Bear Cub, fold a Water-Bomb Base. Fold both upper-lying wings to the middle line, and then undo the prefolds again.

4. Crease the left, upper wing up to the prefold. Open this crease and…

5. …firmly press the fold into a Squash Fold. On the dashed lines…

6. …fold the back-paw point that appears upward. Bring a small corner inward and fold the paw downward again.

7. Repeat steps **4** to **6** with the right wing on the back of the figure. Fold the wing of the Water-Bomb Base to the side so that you can make the forelegs.

8. Fold the right wing to the middle line. Open this wing and fold the point inward along the dashed line. On the dashed line, fold the front paw…

9. …upward and then again downward. Make the left foreleg in the same way, and set up the figure so that the front paws lie flat on the ground. Attach the head of the Bear Cub at any angle you wish to one of the front legs of the body.

Tip: If you use black and white paper instead of brown, you get the Polar Bears that you see in the With the Penguins scene.

Big Panda **

Basic Shape: Shawl Fold
Paper: Two-color origami paper,
e.g., black/white
Size: 6″

	Body	15 cm
	Head	

Body

1. Fold the paper for the body twice diagonally in the middle. The black side lies inside.

2. Open the figure, and bring one corner to the middle.

3. Fold this corner outward again. On the dashed line…

4. …bring the opposite corner inward.

5. Close the figure diagonally. On the dashed line…

6. …fold the edges on both sides of the figure outward. Then, on the dashed line…

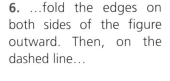

7. …turn the small corners on both sides of the figure inward. That is the body of the Big Panda.

Head

8. Fold the paper for the head diagonally in the middle. The black side faces up.

9. Bring both points along the edges in a downward direction. Along the dashed line…

10. …fold a small corner downward. Then, along this corner,…

11. …both points are folded upward once more.

12. Turn the figure over and, on the dashed line,…

13. …fold the lower corner upward. Then, undo this fold, and on the dashed line…

14. …fold the lower corner upward. Cut the eye rings in along this fold,

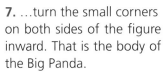

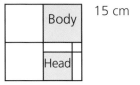

15. Undo all other folds again by opening up the figure. Fold the paper in the other diagonal direction.

16. Cut out a slight half-cross shaped piece.

17. Refold the figure, as you did before, and then fold the small white corner between the ears towards the back.

18. Fold the points of the ears inward and the tip of the nose upward. That is the head of both the Big as well as the Little Panda. Paste the head onto the body at any angle.

Little Panda ✳✳✳

Basic Shape: Shawl Fold, Water-Bomb Base
Paper: Two-color origami paper,
        e.g., black/white
Size: 6″   15 cm

Body	Head

1. Make the head for Little Panda in exactly the same way you did for the Big Panda. The body is formed from the Water-Bomb Base; the only difference is that, this time, at the beginning of the Water-Bomb Base the white side faces down!

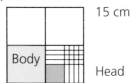

2. Open the Water-Bomb Base, and fold the two lower corners to the middle. Undo this fold again and …

3. …bring half of both lower sides inward.

4. Fold both diagonal edges inward.

5. Refold the figure once again into the shape of the Water-Bomb Base.

6. Open the back triangle of the Water-Bomb Base by laying it out into a square on the left side of the figure.

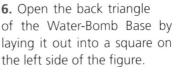

7. Fold the left, upper corner forward up to the point of the black corner. Open this fold once more…

8. …and make a Sink Fold on this preliminary crease. Fold on the dashed line…

9. …the back edges to the front on both sides of the figure. This is the body of Little Panda.

Fir Tree **

Basic Shape: Water-Bomb Base, Fan
Paper: Origami paper, e.g., green and brown
Size: 6" 15 cm
(2 green,
1 brown)

Trunk
Treetop

1. Make a Water-Bomb Base.

2. Fold the forward left wing to the middle line.

3. Open the wing and firmly push it from the middle into a Squash Fold.

4. Refold the right half of the Squash again on the left side of the figure.

5. Repeat steps **2** to **4** with the forward right wings on the right side of the figure.

6. Turn the figure over and repeat the folds of steps **2** to **5** on the back of the figure.

7. Open the figure. On the dashed lines…

8. …bring the four corners on the inside toward the center for a simple Fir.

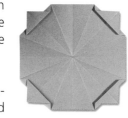

9. …Close the figure into a Fir. All Valley Folds touch each other on the inside of the middle of the figure.

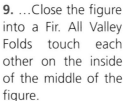

10. Several such treetops can be folded as well as pasted one on top of each other for even higher Firs.

11. For a Fir with a trunk, the corners are folded on the dashed lines as in step **7** from the outside inward and then out again. Close the figure into a treetop as described in step **10**.

12. For the trunk, make a 16-fold Fan. Glue the Fan together, at the two outer strips as shown so that you get a round trunk. Place or paste the treetop onto the trunk.

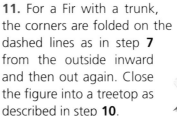

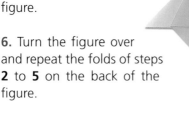

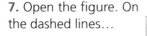